Meet Heidi, the Only Woman Ever Declared User-Friendly by IBM!

Learn all about Heidi Abromowitz in a book based not only on fact but also on rumor, innuendo, and graffiti! To wit:

- Baby Heidi, who cut her teeth on the pop-up version of *The Story of O*
- Camper Heidi, who was first at mail call—until she discovered that all they were handing out were letters
- High School Heidi, who bent over backward to put a smile on the faces of the glee club
- Candy Striper Heidi, who gave mouth-to-mouth resuscitation a bad name
- Career Girl Heidi, busily discovering what "The Peter Principle" was all about
- Heidi, the International Relations pro, involved in more undercover operations than the CIA

Now, in a last-ditch effort to pay off her mortgage, America's number-one comedienne lays aside—for money—her childhood vow of confidence to tell the complete, uncensored story. You may be shocked, awed, or even inspired by . . .

The Life and (Hard) Times of

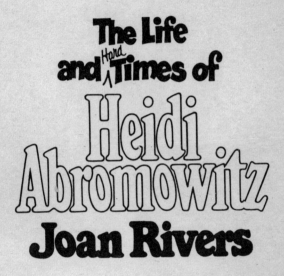

Heidi Abromowitz

Joan Rivers

Illustrations Created and Designed by
James Sherman

A DELL BOOK

Published by
Dell Publishing Co., Inc.
1 Dag Hammarskjold Plaza
New York, New York 10017

Dell ® TM 681510, Dell Publishing Co., Inc.

ISBN: 0-440-14721-2

Reprinted by arrangement with Delacorte Press
Printed in the United States of America
First Dell printing—December 1985
OPM

To all the employees of the Cannon sheet company, who worked beyond the call of duty to fulfill Heidi's mail orders.

ACKNOWLEDGMENTS

I'd like to express my sincere thanks to the numerous organizations and individuals whose candor and cooperation helped enormously in the preparation of this book, especially the men of the United States Armed Forces, the National Football League, the American Football League, those great kids at the Atlanta Center for Disease Control, the World Health Organization, the late Sir Sandford Fleming, the Vienna Boys Choir, the Larchmont Free Clinic, Dr. Paul Ehrlich, the Boy Scouts of America, the Secaucus Men's Bowling League, the French Foreign Legion, the guys at Paul's garage... and Hester Mundis.

CONTENTS

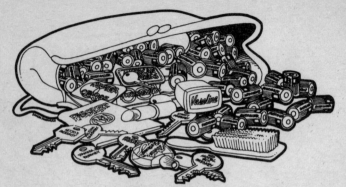

Section Three: Making It

You show me a woman with a naturally beautiful body, and I'll show you a tramp!

—JOAN RIVERS

The Life
and Times of
Heidi
Abromowitz

INTRODUCTION

Can we talk? When someone mentions the name of Heidi Abromowitz, words such as "virtuous," "chaste," "honorable," "moral," and "upright" never come to mind.

The girl was a tramp from the moment her mother's water broke. You think I'm kidding? When the doctor spanked her at birth, she cried for more!

Still, we grew up together as friends, and over the years she confided in me, entrusted to me details of her life that I gave my sacred vow *never* to reveal.

But last month, after I'd caught her in the bushes with my German shepherd for the third time (he's the only dog in Beverly Hills being treated for herpes!), a publisher phoned and offered me big bucks for Heidi's story.

I thought about my sacred vow.

I thought about my dog's vet bill.

I sold out like a shot.

Here then, written for the lay reader, is *The Life and Hard Times of Heidi Abromowitz,* an uncensored, unauthorized biography of the girl whose come-hither look inspired the discovery of penicillin; a book based not only on fact but also on rumor, innuendo, and graffiti from walls of phone booths and men's rooms around the world.

SECTION ONE
The Early Years

CHAPTER I
*Never put off for tomorrow
who you can put out for tonight.*
—*HEIDI ABROMOWITZ*

BABY BIMBO ABROMOWITZ

*E*veryone in Larchmont knew that Heidi was a tramp the day she came home from the hospital. At that point in her life it wasn't the rubber pants that gave her away, or even the fact that when someone picked her up for burping, she blew in his ear. Let me put it this way: She did things with her pacifier that most women still haven't done with their husbands. Is that a tramp, or what?

It was almost unthinkable that we would ever become friends, especially to *my* mother. She considered anyone who wore open-toed shoes an exhibitionist.

Heidi and I were *so* unalike. I mean, when I had diaper rash, she had herpes. I'd fuss about going to bed; she'd hit the mattress the minute someone un-

zipped her bunting. I slept with stuffed animals; she slept with real ones. You get the picture.

Heidi stayed different from the rest of us. She never went through a *no* phase (her first words were "Sure, sailor!"), never sucked her thumb if she could suck someone else's, and when she waved "bye-bye," it was with her panties.

Even before she was toilet-trained, that tramp's name was on bathroom walls!

On the other hand, both of us did like bedtime stories and books—of course, not the same ones. While I was still pointing to pictures in "Goldilocks and the Three Bears," she was reading the pop-up version of *The Story of O*.

11

CHAPTER II

*The early bird catches the
worm—but that's a lot better
than herpes.*

—HEIDI ABROMOWITZ

TODDLER TRAMP

Before we even entered kindergarten, Heidi was raising eyebrows as often as her skirt. Think I'm exaggerating? Well, how many four-year-olds do you know who've had their birthday parties raided by the police? I'm serious! She jumped out of her own birthday cake!

My mother never let me go to any of Heidi's parties after I told her about the one where we played Simon Says with a whip. (Simon says, "DO THIS! DO THAT!") She'd probably *never* have let me see Heidi again if I'd told where that preschooler pop-tart had hidden the marshmallows for the treasure hunt!

Like men in later years, Heidi's toys said a lot about her; all of it unprintable. Her dollhouse had a

red light on it! Her coloring books had dirty pictures! She was the only kid in the neighborhood who had an anatomically correct G.I. Joe doll—*and it was battery-operated*!

She also had an advanced Erector set. What she did with that is better left unmentioned.

CHAPTER III

Jack, be nimble, Jack, be quick.
That's fifty dollars for this trick.

—HEIDI ABROMOWITZ

THE ELEMENTARY PIECE

*O*nce we entered elementary school, there were no longer any doubts (as if there ever had been) about what Heidi was. The very first day she got up and recited the alphabet "A-B-V-D" and then for show and tell she took off her dress.

In all fairness, though, she did work and play well with others—but she charged for it. She'd put out for a nickel, a dime, or a quarter and gave a whole new meaning to the term "loose change." At six, she was already delivering faster than Federal Express.

Then again, she wasn't always a good sport. When she found out that the game was "London Bridge is [not London *britches*] falling down," she refused to play.

But she did want a part in our second-grade production of "Snow White and the Seven Dwarfs." *Obviously* she wasn't going to be Snow White, so they created a role for her. They added an extra dwarf—called Easy.

By the time Heidi and I entered third grade the differences between us became even more obvious. She developed faster than a Polaroid. One day nothing. The next, bazoom-bazooms. She couldn't see her flash cards.

That was a big turning point. She became so trampy that her parents used to ask her, "What did you earn in school today?" Before we were in sixth grade, that girl was taking Flintstone's chewable birth control pills.

I'm telling you that at eight she knew more about reproduction than Xerox. While I was just learning the facts of life, she was teaching them! My first question about sex was "Where did I come from?" Hers was "Was it good for you, too?"

I once asked her, "Don't you know the wages of sin?" and she said, "Sure. Fifty bucks for the whole night."

"I mean, haven't you ever thought of being chaste?"

"Of course," she said, "all the time—especially by a football team."

So there I was, home learning the fifty states while she was being transported across their lines. My mother used to say to me, "Don't worry, she'll have to pay the piper." Oh, yeah? She was twelve years old and the piper was paying her!

Kissed a boy for the first time today. Very disappointing. It's nothing compared to oral sex.

CHAPTER IV

The grass is always greener on the other side of the fence. So if you don't want to stain your skirt, do it on this side.

—HEIDI ABROMOWITZ

THE TRAMP AT CAMP

The year we went to camp, I was such a bow wow that my parents had considered sending me to obedience school instead. But Heidi was in full bloom and ready for all the open-air cross-pollination she could get. While we were still on the bus, someone who was into astrology asked her what her sign was, and she said, "Yield!"

Right away she was the first one at mail call—until she discovered that all they were handing out were letters. But I'm telling you, before one week had gone by, she could get any guy up before reveille and in bed before lights out. Her tent had a turnstile!

In the water she was anything but *aqua-pure*. I was still learning the doggie paddle while she was teaching counselors the breast stroke—and the bitch couldn't even swim!

Where team sports were involved, she was a natural. She'd play ball with anyone. Contact sports were where she excelled. By the end of the summer she had tackled every guy who was game.

In arts and crafts, while we made plant holders, she was making macramé diaphragms!

She was such a slut that her idea of being prepared for a hike was wearing an air mattress.

Oh, and at cookouts? She was the hit of every one. She could start a campfire just by rubbing her thighs together.

I remember all this vividly because that was the year the infirmary used up its entire supply of penicillin.

Probably what I remember most is that the day we were to board the buses for home we all marched down the road together—except for Heidi, who followed the path of least resistance.

SECTION TWO

The Harlot in High School

CHAPTER V

*Anyone who believes that only
time will tell has never been
in a boys' locker room.*
—*HEIDI ABROMOWITZ*

TEEN TART

When we entered high school, Heidi was instantly voted The Girl Most Likely To. The reasons were obvious.

Both of them.

In a sweater she looked like a walking dairy state. I was more underdeveloped than most third world nations. My training bra had taught me nothing, while hers had been an overachiever!

We both joined the drama club at the same time. She immediately got the lead in *Once upon a Mattress;* I got it in *Call Me Mister.* Talk about typecasting!

I wouldn't go so far as to say that Heidi wasn't productive in school, but in shop class the only thing she made was the teacher.

Then again, she did take on an all-boys' astronomy class and gave them a deeper understanding

of the big bang theory. And in physics she was able to prove that perpetual motion really did exist. None of this, of course, stopped her from getting in trouble. Once she was sent to the principal's office. She stayed there for three days!

At the end of our freshman year she joined the band. At first she played the rape whistle but gave it up when the turnout didn't stand up to her expectations. That's when she became a majorette, the only one whose baton took two D-cell batteries.

That slut had so many vibrators her bedroom sounded like a construction site!

When the term ended, she was voted the Girl Most Likely to Go Down in History...and French...and Social Studies...and Math...and... Need I say more?

During summer recess she joined a traveling carnival as a ride.

CHAPTER VI

*Never get into a car with
bucket seats—unless there's
champagne in the buckets.*

—*HEIDI ABROMOWITZ*

DATING DAZE
OF THE
SOPHOMORE SLUT

*W*hen Heidi had her braces removed, the entire
football team sent her orthodontist a thank-you
note. She was so popular with those guys they
wanted to build a memorial to her under the sta-
dium. She used to hang out in their locker room
and play checkers just so she could say, "Jump
me!"

I'm telling you, this girl was a TRAMP! Sure she
was popular. Her bra size was the same as her IQ—
40. I was so flat I used to put *X*'s on my chest and
write, "You are here." (For a while I considered
having "Play other side" tattooed on my back.) I
wore angora sweaters just so the guys would have
something to pet.

Heidi had boyfriends by the score—and, believe
me, all of them did! She thought "going steady"

meant marathon sex. Her idea of a double date was two guys and herself. An intimate evening was spending the night with just *one* fraternity.

She invented the ménage-à-gang.

Do you think I'm bitter? You're right. I am! That tramp had dates all the time. She used to put mirrors on her own shoes (and she had the same pair for four years without the soles even getting scuffed). Her legs were apart so often they were pen pals.

She had a Murphy bed in her gym locker!

By midterm everyone was calling her Bounty because she was the quicker picker-upper.

She once had sex with eighteen guys in the back seat of a car—and that's while it was still in the showroom! She was twenty-four before she realized you could also use a car to drive in and that front seats weren't optional.

Her bedroom was decorated like the inside of a '63 Chevy just so that she'd feel at home. You had to climb over the front seat to get to her bed. She told me that the only way she could get really comfortable was to lie on her back with her feet out the window.

When she felt particularly kinky, she covered the bed with potato chips and called herself the Frito Lay.

Heidi went to the movies more than any other girl I knew, and saw fewer of them than Helen Keller.

In Larchmont no one ever had to ask what was playing at the theater; the answer was always "Heidi."

She was also the regular coming attraction.

She was the only girl I knew who ever worried about popcorn stains on the back of her skirt.

But she loved the movies, probably because she didn't have to get up to turn out the lights, and of all her unwatched films, the following were her favorites:

HEIDI'S ALL-TIME FAVORITE FLICKS

- IN THE HEAT OF THE NIGHT
- AFFAIR WITH A STRANGER
- ALL THE KING'S MEN
- ALL THE YOUNG MEN
- LOVE IS A MANY-SPLENDORED THING
- A MAN FOR ALL SEASONS
- THE DIRTY DOZEN
- EASY RIDER
- ALL THE PRESIDENT'S MEN
- ALL THIS AND HEAVEN TOO
- ANY NUMBER CAN PLAY
- ANYTHING GOES

In some ways, Heidi was a paradox; in others, just a tramp. She didn't care much for singing, but in high school she bent over backwards to put a smile on the faces of the glee club.

Musically inclined or not, she had some songs that everyone associated with her:

HEIDI'S ALL-TIME HIT PARADE

- "SATISFACTION"
- "NOBODY DOES IT BETTER"
- "HELP ME MAKE IT THROUGH THE NIGHT"
- "GOOD VIBRATIONS"
- "I'M NEVER SATISFIED"
- "FEELINGS"
- "LET THE GOOD TIMES ROLL"
- "LET'S GET PHYSICAL"
- "THE LADY IS A TRAMP"
- "BLOWIN' IN THE WIND"

HEIDI'S DATING NO-NOs

- Never let a guy get away with kissing you on the first date if you can get him to do more.

- Never get into S&M with a guy who wears imitation leather.

- Never admit to being older than your bra size.

- Never floss with a stranger.

- Never take an out-of-state check.

CHAPTER VII

*A fool and his money are soon
parted—which is why I never
go out with a guy whose IQ is
over fifty.*

—HEIDI ABROMOWITZ

SENIOR STRUMPET

In our senior year Heidi visited a lot of universities; she tried to offer herself as a student loan. It was interesting, because around the same time we'd both decided we were going to give our bodies to the Harvard Medical School—only *I* was going to wait until I was dead.

Heidi never waited for anything.

By that point she was coming into heat faster than a microwave. She'd gotten pinned so many times I figure she was probably the first American to get acupuncture. She was taking the morning-after pill twice a night and buying early pregnancy tests in six-packs.

She was buying Vaseline in decorator colors.

Her yearbook photo was a foldout.

I mean, we're talking *tramp*! On the golf course when someone yelled, "Fore," she'd shout, "Play." Her mouth was considered a recreational vehicle. She used Lysol as a moisturizer!

But damn it, that bitch got a wrist corsage for the prom, and all I got was a flea collar with a daisy.

Graduation was really memorable. Heidi's parents, even though they came in dark glasses and wigs, were proud of her. They told her that they were throwing out her baby shoes and having her first diaphragm bronzed instead. She was thrilled—especially since it had been her old Hula-Hoop.

What I remember most vividly, though, is that when the rest of the class was going up for their diplomas, Heidi was going down.

Went to the Vatican today and met the pope. When he came up to me, I did what everyone else was doing and dropped to my knees.

Boy, what a commotion! How the hell did I know it was his ring I was supposed to kiss?

CHAPTER VIII

*One good turn deserves
another...and another...and another...*

—*HEIDI ABROMOWITZ*

THE
BROAD
ABROAD

After graduation Heidi got a passport stamped with the surgeon general's warning and took off for a grand tour of Europe.

Well, it wasn't a *grand* grand tour. Heidi couldn't care less about any accommodations that she herself didn't provide. Let me put it this way, the ship was a tramp steamer, and her stateroom was so far below deck that the last person to occupy it had been Kunta Kinte.

Still, this didn't faze Heidi. That girl had a great way of making friends, and strangers, and anyone else who was around. She just hung out a Please Disturb sign, lay back, and enjoyed the pleasure of her fellow travelers' company.

STRIKING OUT IN THE BRITISH EMPIRE

Heidi's first stop was England. After an hour of going through customs, the officials unanimously thanked her for coming across. She told them not to mention it, and slipped them another half an hour to insure it.

After that she set out for London, where she suffered one of the major disappointments of her life: She learned that Big Ben was a clock.

Trooper tart that she was, she took this in her stride, along with several bobbies, two palace guards and a cross dresser who called himself Boy/Girl George.

It didn't take long for Heidi to find out that the British had a lot more to offer than stiff upper lips. Unfortunately she made this discovery with a lamppost in a London fog and was hauled into Old Bailey for soliciting a public utility. As she told me later, "I could have beat the rap if I hadn't made advances to the judge. Who knew it was a woman under that wig?"

Before she left the country, she managed to give a command performance at the House of Lords and a whole new meaning to the term "bed and breakfast."

I'm having an affair with the seventeenth in line to the throne. He wants to marry me, but the sex is dismal. The only way I get through it is by thinking that if the plague ever hits London again, I could be queen ..... But then again, I'm afraid that so could he.

FLAUNTING IT IN FRANCE

The moment Heidi arrived in Paris she was abducted by a regiment of French legionnaires. They knew her by reputation only and wanted to find out if she lived up to it.

Of course she did. But let me tell you, along with everything else that girl had chutzpah. In the midst of that Franco-bango she asked the twelfth legionnaire, "Think I'm easy?"

Heidi was reluctant to leave Paris for a number of reasons—most of them male. (As she'd say later, "Why they call that place Gay Paree *I'll* never know.")

After only one week she had learned to open a bottle of wine and a jar of Vaseline with her toes (a skill that would serve her and many others in later years), and she had developed a crush on the Eiffel Tower. When she found out that she couldn't take it home as a souvenir, she was heartsick.

Page from Heidi's diary, written during her graduation trip to Europe

Saw Versailles this afternoon. Wow, those mirrors are fabulous. What a waste to put them all in the <u>Hall</u>!

MAKING IT IN MONTE CARLO

Before Heidi even entered a casino, she was the odds-on favorite across the board—and borders—of this principality, and believe me it wasn't due to luck. (When I traveled there with my husband Edgar, he took the first tip he got from a dealer and drew a "Don't Pass" line across our sheets.)

Surprisingly, though, Heidi was unimpressed by her visit here. I suspect this was partly due to the fact that there were only three conventions in town at the time—all of them women's auxiliary groups.

It could also have been because Heidi wasn't the gambling type. When she played the slot machines, cherries never came up.

As it turned out, all she played in Monte Carlo was stud poker.

Page from Heidi's diary, written during her graduation trip to Europe

Overheard two guys in the casino bar say, "Once you uncork her, she's earthy, got the right kind of body, and yet is still just a little tart." I immediately tossed them my room key. They tossed it back! Who knew they were talking about a bottle of wine?

IRRESISTING IN ITALY

Venice was first on Heidi's Italian itinerary and foremost in her later fantasies. Few things gave her more pleasure than having those handsome gondoliers paddle her wherever and whenever she wanted them to.

Pisa was her next stop, but the world-famous tower turned out to be a crushing blow to her ego. A frustrating first. After she'd climbed it twice, she was furious it wasn't standing erect.

She chalked it up as an international misunderstanding and headed off for Rome.

Heidi had heard, "When in Rome, do as the Romans do," and, boy, did she ever! What went on in her hotel room made Nero's orgies look like Tupperware parties.

She'd put out for anyone who threw three coins in a fountain.

While she was there she saw more action in the Colosseum than Spartacus and more ceilings than Michelangelo.

By the time she'd left, every restaurant in the city had a dessert named after her. They called it tartalini.

Page from Heidi's diary, written during her graduation trip to Europe

Finally got to Germany.
Deutschland,
        Shmeutschland,
what a drag. If I hadn't
gotten to see those
sausage factories, I
would have been bored
to death.

REIGNING IN SPAIN

The first thing that Heidi did upon arriving in Madrid was to go to the bullring and get a front-row seat. The matador took one look at her and asked for a date. She took one look at the bull and asked if they could double.

As it turned out, they did. Heidi said that she had a great time but couldn't shake the feeling that at the moment of truth the bull was faking it.

"Still," she said later, "it was my kind of country. I like a place where you can go to bed in the middle of the afternoon and no one asks any questions."

GROOVING IN GREECE

I knew that Larchmont's little roundheels wasn't into history, but I still find it hard to believe that all she wanted to do in the country that had spawned Alexander, Zorba, and Formula 44 was to straddle Mount Olympus and have a night alone with the Colossus of Rhodes.

COMING HOME

When Heidi arrived back in New York, the immigration officer asked if she had anything to declare.

"You'll get nothing from me without a strip search," said she.

The officer took her at her word.

It was the highlight of Heidi's grand tour.

SECTION THREE

SECTION THREE

Making It

CHAPTER IX

*Any woman who fakes orgasms too
often winds up not knowing
whether she's coming or going.*
—HEIDI ABROMOWITZ

GOING DOWN
THE AISLE AND
OTHER PLACES

The first time Heidi got married (those tramps always do), a couple of us got together a few weeks before the wedding and told her that we were going to give her a shower (which, God knows, she needed).

We also told her to make a list of things that she wanted, because it was awfully hard to think of something for someone who's had everyone.

For an odd reason, probably the same one that makes people save gum wrappers or used Band-Aids, I've hung on to the list. I think it not only speaks for itself but says a lot about Heidi.

HEIDI'S WEDDING GIFT LIST

Eveready batteries
A Roto-Rooter gift certificate
Sterling silver Vaseline dispenser
An answering machine that only says "yes"
Rubber sheets
Ziploc lingerie
Battery-operated rolling pin
A nonstopwatch
Contraceptive toothpaste
Leather pantyhose
Innerspring underwear
A season pass to the Los Angeles Raiders'
    locker room

I don't know what gifts she actually received; they all came in plain brown wrappers. But I do know that she had her wedding gown designed by Sealy.

I remember asking her, "Who's your best man?"

"I can't decide," she said. "They were all good."

I'll bet they were. The night before the wedding she entertained twenty-five of them! She was having her going-out-of-business sale.

The day of the ceremony she assured me that she loved Edgar only in a brotherly way. (Remind me to tell you about her relationship with her brother sometime.)

Anyway, her big event did take place, and I was there. You could tell it was Heidi's wedding all right; the pews had paper strips on them saying, "Sanitized for your safety."

Now, I'm not against sex before marriage, but *two minutes before*? When the organist played "Here Comes the Bride," Heidi did.

During the ceremony when they got to the part where you're supposed to say, "I do," she said, "I already did," and there wasn't anyone there who doubted her.

The reception was small, but she did have a wedding cake made especially for the occasion. The bride on the top was bowlegged.

When she left for her honeymoon, we all threw wild rice—except for a few sore losers who, I believe, threw penicillin.

Old habits die hard, and I learned later that on her wedding night, when her husband asked her to take off her bra, she said, "That'll be three bucks more." But at least *she* had a good time on her honeymoon. The only fun I had on mine was when I douched with shampoo and blew bubbles.

Oh, I also learned later that she had given all the ushers at her wedding the same thing—the clap.

OUTSPOKEN ABROMOWITZISMS
HEIDI'S OPINIONS
ON

The Women's Movement

"It's best from the waist down."

The Right to Life

"Anyone who subscribes certainly deserves it."

Arms Control

"Why bother, unless you're being squeezed too tightly?"

Food Stamps

"They taste terrible, and I never know what wine to serve with them."

Energy Conservation

"I'm all for it—especially if I'm having more than one guy a night."

ERA

"It works pretty well as a laundry detergent."

The Space Program

"I never watch it."

Artificial Insemination

"It's nothing compared to the real thing."

The Labor Movement

"I'd say that Lamaze is the way to go."

Private Enterprise

"He's probably okay, but I prefer Captain Kirk."

The Right to Bear Arms

"Arms? You should have the right to expose *any* part of your body!"

Police Brutality

"Could be fun if it's between consenting adults."

The Hite Report

"Looking into length would make a more interesting study."

HEIDI'S _un_ DRESS FOR SUCCESS GUIDELINES

Never

...wear any latex or rubber undergarment except for recreational purposes.

...wear handcuffs with plaid.

...let a panty line show around your ankles.

...expose an erogenous zone without getting the money first.

...wear Odor-Eaters any place but in your shoes.

...underestimate the hazards of a zipper.

...wear designer shields.

...buy a fur from a veterinarian.

...wear anything that leaves something to the imagination.

...put a smoke alarm between your thighs.

Always

...Scotchgard your underwear.

...wear flame-retardant pantyhose.

...wear something leather. ·

...put coin-operated zippers on your jeans.

...remember that wearing less will get you more.

...wear shoes that you can kick off easily.

...wear Velcro-fastening clothes.

...wear your partner out first.

CHAPTER X

*Two is company. Three
is fifty dollars.*
—HEIDI ABROMOWITZ

CAREER
CHIPPY

After her marriage failed, Heidi had herself listed in the Yellow Pages under "Public Utility" and set out to find work. She was determined to find out what the "Peter Principle" was all about.

For a while she took a job as a dentist's assistant, just so she could hear him say, "Open wide." That kept her happy for a while, but when the novelty, nitrous, and a few other things wore off, she had her thighs realigned and moved on.

Not surprisingly, the moment that tramp hit the streets she got a lot of offers. Some were even for jobs.

Consumer Reports asked her to rate Vaseline.

But Heidi wanted to enter the medical field. Having already made bedsores a way of life, she felt she

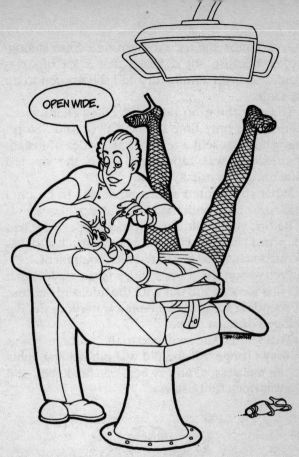

OPEN WIDE.

had experience. Well, no argument there.

Anyway, she became a candy striper. It didn't work out. After only two days on the job she gave mouth-to-mouth resuscitation a bad name. You think I'm kidding? I'm telling you, this venereal vendor had the clap so often that doctors used to treat her for applause! When she left town, four free clinics went out of business!

And dumb? She tried to become a court stenographer because she'd heard that a lot of cases wound up with a hung jury and she wanted to do the same.

The one thing no one ever called Heidi was a quitter. The only time that slut ever said "Stop" was when she sent a telegram. Her idea of instant gratification was rape. And when she wanted something, she usually got it.

What she wanted at this point was to be on a first-name basis with the Seventh Fleet.

Before you could say "Up periscope!" she had the word "next" tattooed on her stomach and was deducting her bed as home-office equipment.

Pretty soon she'd been with so many sailors that her lips went in and out with the tide, and because of spending so much time on a waterbed, she developed dishpan back.

That's when she switched to the air force. It was an easy change. All she did was put landing lights on her mattress, a runway between her knees, and she was open for business.

It was around this time that I lost touch with Heidi; I was probably the only one. Word on the street had it that she'd ventured into the literary world, and if I know Heidi, it was probably by going *under* the transom.

While researching this book, I managed to find a copy of the condensation of her unpublished best seller, *Abromowitz Aerobics,* exercises designed to turn any pelvis into a playground.

I also uncovered what had only been rumored to. exist: Heidi's long-suppressed *Playboy* interview and her much coveted data sheet.

ABROMOWITZ AEROBICS

Beginner's Pickup

(Benefits: by looking ready and willing, you'll be able to eliminate the risk of being mistaken for a tired jogger, substantially increasing the number and scope of all propositions and easily doubling your nightly intake and output.)

- Lean up against a wall, pole, or streetlight.
- Keep legs firmly apart, push out chest, and slouch.
- Lower eyelids so that you look only half awake or totally drunk.
- Repeat exercise six times on each side of the street.

Advanced Pickup

(Benefits: an enlarged clientele and an upwardly mobile income of professional proportions.)

- Same as Beginner's Pickup, only done in Times Square.
- Repeat as often as profitable.

Trickier Thighs in Thirty Seconds

(Benefits: provides an intensified vise grip that's useful for all indoor and outdoor sports, including polo, broncobusting, and workouts with high-tech appliances.)

- Lie down next to a bag of walnuts.
- Bend knees, and plant feet firmly on mattress.
- Put nut between knees, and P-R-E-S-S together until nut cracks.
- Crack as many nuts as you can without getting bored or hungry.

Pelvic Push-ups

(Benefits: a lower torso with a social life of its own.)

- Lie on back.
- Imagine Tom Selleck being lowered from the ceiling—and stopping halfway.
- Raise hips, and try to reach Tom Selleck.
- Keep trying until you lose interest—or until Tom Selleck turns into either Truman Capote or the Elephant Man.

Booby Prizes

(Benefits: larger breasts attract men, enhance sweaters, and keep crumbs out of your lap.)

- With elbows at your sides, exhale vigorously into a balloon.
- Inflate and tie.
- Repeat exercise with another balloon.
- Stuff both into bra.

Heavy Breathing
(Benefits: aids in arousing your partner, showing off your cleavage, faking orgasms, and making obscene phone calls.)
- Grasp a mattress firmly, and flip it over.
- Repeat until you're panting and your panting sounds like a Lamaze mother in labor or a Saint Bernard that's just crossed the Sahara.

Tongue Toners
(Benefits: prevents cellulite on your taste buds, and besides, lazy tongues make lousy lovers.)
- Repeat rapidly six times: "Lascivious little Lolita loves licking long lemon lollipops."
- Never use a sponge for moistening envelopes or stamps.
- Take an all-day sucker to work or bed with you.

Instant Tummy Flatteners
- Orson Welles
- Meatloaf
- Jackie Gleason
- Peter Ustinov
- Luciano Pavarotti

General Tips
- Spend as much time as possible horizontally.
- Keep regular bedtimes (twice a night for best results).
- Always remember that there are two things that should never meet—the twain and your knees.

I HEARD ARI HAD THE BIGGEST. THE ONLY THING BIG ABOUT IT WAS MY DISAPPOINTMENT! | I'LL TRY ANYTHING TWICE. | NOW?! YES!!

PLAYBOY INTERVIEW:
HEIDI ABROMOWITZ

A titillating talk with America's top tramp

Anyone who hasn't heard of Heidi Abromowitz is either still in diapers or clinically dead. The youngest woman to ever enter the world's oldest profession, she has served tirelessly under every administration since Eisenhower's in capacities too numerous to mention.

IBM has certified her "User Friendly," Eveready has voted her its "Girl of the Year" for more than two decades, and she has the distinction of being the only woman ever to have her tongue insured by Lloyds of London.

Probably the most renowned tramp since Charlie Chaplin, her starring role in numerous army training films has earned her the reputation she so rightly deserves.

She has been rumored to be the mysterious Deep Throat mentioned in the Watergate investigation, and her name has more than once been romantically linked with the Washington Monument.

We finally caught up with Heidi, for this interview, in a Winnebago parked behind a bowling alley in Secaucus, New Jersey.

PLAYBOY: There have been a lot of derogatory, insulting, and unprintable remarks made about you. How many of these are *really* true?

ABROMOWITZ: All of them.

PLAYBOY: You admit that you're a tramp?

ABROMOWITZ: Admit it? I can give you references.

PLAYBOY: When did you realize that this was the way you would leave your mark on the world?

ABROMOWITZ: After the first guy I kissed developed a rash.

PLAYBOY: You grew up in a small town, didn't you?

ABROMOWITZ: Small? Larchmont was so small

that our town dump was a Hefty bag. The sign on our McDonald's said, "Over 4 Served." Our volunteer fire department was two guys with squirt guns. Our bakery didn't even make layer cakes. If three people got the flu, it was an epidemic. During the summer we had a pet mosquito. The only twenty-four-hour service available was me!

PLAYBOY: Is that why you got your reputation so early in life?

ABROMOWITZ: You bet. In Larchmont all you had to do was pack some Vaseline, a black nightgown, and a pair of handcuffs in your lunch pail, and—*bang!*—right away you were a tramp.

PLAYBOY: It's been said that you went through a phase where you dated only baseball players. Why was that?

ABROMOWITZ: I was into guys who'd play ball with me. The way I figured, if they could get to first base, they deserved to score.

PLAYBOY: You've also dated football players.

ABROMOWITZ: I like to play the field.

PLAYBOY: You've been married several times. Do you believe that fidelity is important?

ABROMOWITZ: Only for my stereo.

PLAYBOY: In other words, your marriages suffered from lack of monogamy.

ABROMOWITZ: Lack of monogamy? My bookshelves and coffee table were solid monogamy. And so was my dinette set.

PLAYBOY: Is it true that you spent all your honeymoons at the North Pole?

ABROMOWITZ: Absolutely.

PLAYBOY: Why was that?

ABROMOWITZ: Because the nights were six months long.

PLAYBOY: Based on experience, who do you now feel would wear the pants in your ideal marriage?

ABROMOWITZ: None of us.

PLAYBOY: You've said that you've been involved with many government administrations. In what capacity?

ABROMOWITZ: Mostly international relations and foreign affairs.

PLAYBOY: How did you get involved in those health-related army films?

ABROMOWITZ: I took private lessons.

PLAYBOY: Are you still involved with the military?

ABROMOWITZ: Just on a first come, first served basis.

PLAYBOY: Your life appears to have been filled with ups and downs.

ABROMOWITZ: You can say that again.

PLAYBOY: Have these affected you psychologically?

ABROMOWITZ: Are you kidding? I have more hang-ups than Christina Onassis' answering machine.

PLAYBOY: Could you tell us about them?

ABROMOWITZ: Well, they're phobias.

PLAYBOY: What sort of phobias?

ABROMOWITZ: I don't think they have medical names—yet.

PLAYBOY: Just use lay terms.

ABROMOWITZ: Can you print those?

PLAYBOY: Uh, let's put it another way. What is it that you're frightened of?

ABROMOWITZ: A lot of things.

PLAYBOY: Such as?

ABROMOWITZ: Power failures.

PLAYBOY: Hmmmmm. What else?

ABROMOWITZ: Do Not Enter signs.

PLAYBOY: Hmmmmm.

ABROMOWITZ: Convents.

PLAYBOY: Hmmmmm.

ABROMOWITZ: Body stockings.

PLAYBOY: We get the picture.

ABROMOWITZ: Girl Scout camps.

PLAYBOY: Right. Now—

ABROMOWITZ: Being stranded on a desert island with Billy Graham, Anita Bryant, Marie Osmond, and all four Lennon sisters.

PLAYBOY: Well, aside from these hang-ups, how are you?

ABROMOWITZ: Best on my back.

PLAYBOY: So it's been said.

ABROMOWITZ: Talk is cheap, and so am I.

PLAYBOY: Surely, you're putting us on.

ABROMOWITZ: Like hell I am. Can you break a five?

(Editor's note: This was as far as the interview went—
Heidi went all the way.)

HEIDI'S PLAYMATE
DATA SHEET

NAME: Heidi Abromowitz

BUST: '73 (for performing an unnatural act with a snowblower in Sears' Home & Garden department)

WAIST: Nothing (and want not either)

HIPS: Hips? Hips, hooray!

HEIGHT: Not too short for Kareem and not too tall for Dudley

WEIGHT: Me? Never!

BIRTHDATE: June 7, A.D.

BIRTHPLACE: Same as everyone else's

AMBITION: To serve more than McDonald's

TURN-ONS: Vacancy signs on motels, suction cups, and fly fishing

TURNOFFS: Nothing

FAVORITE MOVIE: *One Bride for Seven Brothers*

FAVORITE FOODS: Hot cross buns, Tootsie Rolls, pigs in blankets, and apple turnovers

FAVORITE PLACE: G spot

IDEAL MAN: *Homo sapiens*

SECRET FANTASIES: To lay the Alaska pipeline and have sex with a parade

CHAPTER XI

*Never let yourself get tied down
to housework if you can get tied
down to a bed instead.*

—HEIDI ABROMOWITZ

HOOKER
HOUSEWIFE

The last time I visited Heidi she'd already had quite a few husbands, a couple of them her own, and had been involved in more undercover operations than the CIA.

It had been a long time, but the moment she opened the door I knew it was her. Despite that Frederick's of Hollywood exterior, I could still see the old trash for cash girl, the tramp I'd grown up with, the woman whose body language would never consist of more than four-letter words.

She was the only person I knew whose idea of a formal evening was putting sheets on the bed.

She was thrilled with the No-Pest strips I'd brought. She thought there were just enough to make a skirt.

The place she was living in was above an army recruiting center near Larchmont, New York. The decor of the apartment could only be described as Tart Deco. I mean, we're talking Slut City. There were more electric appliances in the bedroom than in the kitchen! On an average night she could cause a brownout as far north as Buffalo.

She was living there with her son, who had evidently been named after his father. The kid's name was Trick.

She confessed that she hadn't changed much (which I suspect meant never having to break a bill larger than a twenty) and admitted that even during the ninth month of her pregnancy she had still been sexually active. Well, that was pretty *obvious*! I saw the baby pictures. The kid had more dents than a fender in a body shop!

It was also obvious that motherhood hadn't cramped Heidi's style. While we were talking, the little bump face came into the room and wanted to know when Uncle Dallas Cowboy was coming back to visit.

I changed the subject and asked her what she was up to lately. She said, "Thirty bucks an hour." Let me tell you, I was impressed. I mean, this tramp had more miles on her than the Los Angeles freeways. Her thighs had an off ramp!

Anyway, she said that the years had mellowed her. She told me that lately when she passed a motel, she had a feeling of déjà screw. She also said that she had become more socially conscious. She didn't want to be responsible for any more communicable diseases and therefore was dating only ambassadors, because they had diplomatic immunity.

Then she showed me her little black book. I thought she was bringing out the Encyclopaedia Britannica! She wanted someone to hang on to it for safekeeping and said she couldn't think of anyone it would be safer with than me. Bitch!

Before I left, I asked her if she had made any plans for the future, and she said, "The crew of the space shuttle."

I papered her lips and kissed her good-bye.

Saturday, August 12

Saw T. again tonight. You'd think by this time he wouldn't insist on my calling him "Mister."

He's definitely on my A team, but a flunk out at foreplay. He still just snaps his fingers, points, and says, "Be there!"

Friday, September 4

Well, that's it for Jimmy! He might have one hell of a smile, but in a lot more places than his heart — but I've had it with those goddamn peanut shells in the bed.

Sunday, March 30

Whew! I don't mind quiet types, but that Marcel was _too_ much! The least he could have done was taken off those stupid white gloves!

That's the last blind date I accept through the mail. If he writes again, I'll tell him to mime his _own_ business.

Friday, December 22

Drove to Scarsdale for a scene with Hy the other night. (We had spinach salad, so it must have been Wednesday.)

For a bald, skinny ugly guy he's not bad. As a lover he should be shot.

Tuesday, November 29

Saw Pablo last night. What a difference now that he's out of that goddamn Blue Period! He told me that I was the best thing he'd ever put on canvas. I guess it was worth shlepping that hammock over.

Tuesday, July 17

Good old Al E. stopped by today. (Boy, can he use a shave and haircut. I wouldn't be surprised if they combed his hair and the Lindbergh baby fell out.) I've got to hand it to the guy, though. When he says energy equals mass times the speed of light squared, he's not just whistling theory. I didn't even undress and he was already finished.

Wednesday, July 21

Got back in the saddle with Roy again. It wasn't the same as in the old days when he brought Figs along for kicks.

Poor Roy. I think his bronco busting days are numbered. Good thing he's into fast food, because as far as sex goes, he's headed for the last roundup.

Saturday, February 27

Kinked it up with Claus yesterday, but think that's the last time. I can usually get into any- thing — but come on, the freezer? No wonder his wife's in a coma. You can only fake a headache for so long. I'll lie still for a lot of things — but sex isn't one of them.

Monday, October 24

Went to Graceland today and got all shook up. Old platinum pelvis is turning out to be nothing but a hound dog. I swear if he doesn't shape up, the next time we get together I'm gonna step on his blue svede shoes.

Thursday, January 30.

Saw R yesterday. As usual, I fell asleep when he started to reminisce about that mutt Checkers. I knew I had at least two hours before he got to the Watergate shit.

Boy, I don't know how he ever got the nickname Tricky Dick. All I know is that he won't have me to kick him around any more.

CHAPTER XII
Better laid than never.
—HEIDI ABROMOWITZ

FEMME FINALE

After our last meeting I didn't see Heidi again until she began loitering in the bushes with Bruno, our German shepherd.

I should have suspected that something was up when he acquired a taste for oysters, but I didn't, not even when he started sneaking leashes and cans of vintage Alpo out to the garden. I still might not have guessed what was going on if I hadn't caught Heidi lying next to him, smoking a Milk-Bone.

And then, of course, when that cold sore on Bruno's snout turned out to be something else, well...the rest is history—or at least this book.

So You're Still Not Convinced She's a Tramp?

Oh, yeah? Well, GROW UP!

Hoover classifies her tongue as a vacuum attachment!

Her body has been declared a national recreation area!

Her diaphragms come with service contracts!

She has an IUD with a beeper!

Her rape whistle plays Sinatra tunes!

She uses industrial-strength douche!

Her gynecologist entered her in the Grand Canyon look-alike contest!

Her underwear is by Rubbermaid!

Her pantyhose has a pet door!

She was hospitalized for six months when a truck driver mistook her for the Holland Tunnel!

ABROMOWITZ APPENDIXES

THE ABROMOWITZ BOOK OF
WORLD RECORDS

She's been on her knees more times than
Billy Graham.

*

She's been laid on more kitchen floors than
linoleum.

*

She's had her legs in the air more than
Baryshnikov.

*

She's done more screwing than Black &
Decker.

*

She's had more violations than a parking meter.

*

She's responsible for more merry men than
Robin Hood.

*

She's been involved in more layoffs than GM.

*

She's turned more tricks than Houdini.

*

She's been in more motel rooms than the Bible.

*

She's been boarded more times than Amtrak.

She's been mounted more often than
Trigger.

*

She's been involved with more animals than
Marlin Perkins.

*

She's entertained more troops than Bob Hope.

*

She's been at more bedsides than Dr. Kildare.

*

She's been turned more ways than Rubik's
cube.

*

She's spent more time under men than
barstools.

*

She's seen more traffic than the George
Washington Bridge.

*

She's had more turnovers than the International House of Pancakes.

*

She's been under more sheets than the
Ku Klux Klan.

*

She's had more marines land on her bed
than on Iwo Jima.

BECKY ABROMOWITZ

ALISON DAWN ABROMOWITZ

ABROMOWITZ TRAMPS IN HISTORY

Becky Abromowitz (thirteenth century B.C.)
Egypt's girl most likely to be found in the
bulrushes. Her plan to seduce Moses succeeded
when she found a loophole in the Ten Commandments.

Alison Dawn Abromowitz the Hun (fifth century A.D.)
Camp follower and troop tramp for Attila's barbarous legions. A frequent tent partner of the infamous Hun king, she ran off with a Roman
candlemaker.

Edith Abromowitz (1756–1806)
One of the first ladies of the evening in the colonies. She was George Washington's mistress until
her lips couldn't take any more splinters. She is
probably best known for making a big splash with
her skinny-dipping highjinks at the Boston Tea

EDITH & LIBERTY ABROMOWITZ

FIFI ABROMOWITZ

Party and having privately performed all of the original Intolerable Acts.

Liberty Abromowitz (1757–1809)

Sister of Edith and bed buddy of many of the nation's early patriots. After her on again, off again romance with Ben Franklin fell apart (she's the one who reputedly told him to "go fly a kite"), she and her sister took up with Patrick Henry. Seductresses who earned their Stars and Stripes the old-fashioned way, by working for them, the Abromowitz sisters nearly drove Patrick Henry mad with desire. This is attested to by his famous impassioned (oft-misquoted) cry, "Give me Liberty or give me Edith!"

Fifi Abromowitz (1794–1815)

A notorious, tiny French *pièce de nonrésistance,* Fifi stood no more than twelve inches tall. Napoleon found her irresistible and would often keep her in his shirt pocket, where he could goose her for good luck.

Helga Jennifer Abromowitz (1796–1850)

Often referred to as the Slut of Stuttgart, she was openly intimate with Ludwig van Beethoven, who preferred to call her his little *sacher tart*. Though it is known that Beethoven never heard a word Helga said, it is widely believed that she was partly responsible for his Fifth Symphony and wholly responsible for his sixth case of the clap.

Romaine Wendy Abromowitz (1829–1847)

A footloose, adventurous party girl who would go anywhere for a party, Romaine's reputation was cut short when she headed west with the wrong party —George Donner's. Ironically, she could have made it through the pass if she hadn't been the one vegetarian with the party.

Emmy Pamela Abromowitz (1856–1919)

An enterprising harlot with pioneer gumption and

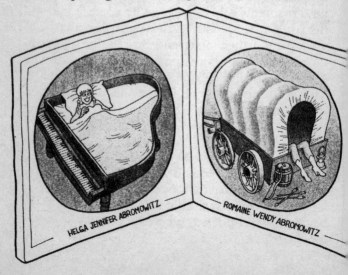

HELGA JENNIFER ABROMOWITZ

ROMAINE WENDY ABROMOWITZ

a trick pelvis, she ran the best little House on the Bighorn. Aside from this, not much about her was noteworthy, except perhaps for the fact that she was General Custer's last one-night stand.

Jocasta Abromowitz (1896–1946)

High-strung and often hysterical, Jocasta was a Viennese call girl who had an obsessive fear of being sexually attracted to her son, Eddy Buzz. An early patient of Sigmund Freud's (her appointments were always before 8:00 A.M.), Jocasta was the first to use Freud's couch for purposes other than analysis. Jocasta and Freud became transactionally attracted to each other. He took to buying her excessive amounts of lingerie—mostly slips. Had he not been determined to protect her identity, he would have named a complex after her. He named it after her son instead, calling it the Eddy-buzz Complex.

EMILY PAMELA ABROMOWITZ

JOCASTA ABROMOWITZ

JAMES SHERMAN

WHAT'S *YOUR* TRAMP POTENTIAL?

Answer the following questions honestly. (If you find yourself cheating or lying, you're obviously a tramp already and don't need to take this test.)

PART ONE

1. If a strange man smiled at you, would you...

- (a) kick him in the groin?
- (b) point out that there was a piece of spinach stuck between his teeth?
- (c) ask for cash and pull him into the nearest phone booth?

2. If a man offered you his seat, would you...

- (a) refuse it?
- (b) take it?
- (c) ask if you could have a better look at it?

3. Do your sexual fantasies ever involve...

- (a) artificial sweeteners?
- (b) wind instruments?
- (c) an MX missile?

4. After lovemaking, do you...

- (a) go to sleep?
- (b) light a cigarette?
- (c) return to the front of the bus?

5. Would it upset you if a date came over for the evening and you were out of...

(a) ice?

(b) Crisco?

(c) the apartment?

6. After having sex, is your biggest worry...

(a) becoming pregnant?

(b) catching a disease?

(c) getting a bad check?

7. Do you consider a long-term relationship...

(a) important?

(b) unnecessary?

(c) anything more than twenty minutes?

8. If you were sexually molested, would you consider...

(a) calling the police?

(b) getting revenge?

(c) sending a bill?

PART TWO

Would You Have Sex:	Yes	No
With another woman's husband?	___	___
...if that woman was your mother?	___	___
On the floor?	___	___
...of the New York Stock Exchange?	___	___
For money?	___	___
...if it's Confederate?	___	___
With an animal?	___	___
...while it's still in a cage?	___	___
With a cucumber?	___	___
...if it's on someone's plate?	___	___

Are You Turned On By:	Yes	No
Seeing a man strip?	___	___
...a piece of furniture?	___	___

The idea of group sex? ____|____

...if the group is the PTA? ____|____

Getting an obscene phone call? ____|____

...if it's a wrong number? ____|____

Are You Willing To:	Yes	No
Try any sexual act at least once?	____	____
...with a jackhammer?	____	____
Go all the way on a first date?	____	____
...to Alaska?	____	____
Fake an orgasm?	____	____
...for your vibrator?	____	____
Suck a man's toes?	____	____
...while his shoes are still on?	____	____

How did you score? See next page.

SO, YOU WANT TO KNOW YOUR TRAMP POTENTIAL? WELL, HERE IT IS!

Answers to Part One:

If you answered (a) to five or more of the questions, you're either under six or Marie Osmond. Your potential for becoming a tramp is about the same as Mother Teresa's.

If you answered (b) to five or more of the questions, you don't have to worry about your reputation. You're safe, you're average, and you're lucky if you can hold on to a man. On the other hand, if you selected (b) in questions 1, 3, 5, and 7, you have latent trampy tendencies and had better watch your step.

If you answered (c) to five or more of the questions and don't know what you are, you're probably the only one. Want me to spell it out for you? You're a T-R-A-M-P, okay? And if you answered (c) to *all* of the questions, you make Heidi Abromowitz look like Mary Poppins.

Answers to Part Two:

Unless you checked *No* for everything, don't worry about your tramp potential. You're a slut.

EPILOGUE

Where is Heidi today? Well, that's anybody's guess and somebody's medical problem.

Rumors have it that she's running her own encounter group on Forty-second Street...teaching oral hygiene at a massage parlor in Tijuana...doing market research for the Hell's Angels...campaigning to get her pelvis designated a Kodak picture spot...has become a basic training program at Fort Bragg.

Rumors also have it that she was sitting on Mount Saint Helens when it erupted.

Whatever the truth, no one ever has to worry about Heidi Abromowitz. If there's one thing I can tell you for certain, no matter what happens, that tramp will always have something to fall back on. *A bed!*